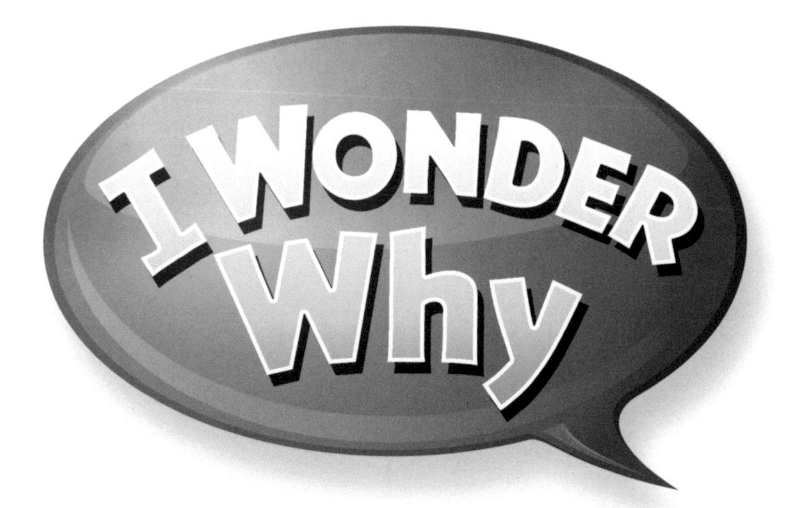

The Sahara Is Cold At Night

and other questions about deserts

Jackie Gaff

Published in the United States by Kingfisher,
175 Fifth Ave., New York, NY 10010
Kingfisher is an imprint of Macmillan Children's Books,
London.

Distributed in the U.S. and Canada by Macmillan,
175 Fifth Ave., New York, NY 10010

Library of Congress Cataloging-in-Publication data has been applied for.

ISBN: 978-0-7534-6797-8

Kingfisher books are available for special promotions and premiums. For details contact: Special Markets Department, Macmillan, 175 Fifth Ave., New York, NY 10010.

For more information, please visit www.kingfisherbooks.com

Printed in China
9 8 7 6 5 4 3 2 1
1TR/0612/UTD/WKT/140MA

Illustrations: James Field (SGA) 5br, 8–9b, 22, 25tr, 27tr, 30–31; Chris Forsey 10–11, 20, 21tl, 8–9; Mike Lacey (SGA) 4–5m, 9tr, 24m, 25b, 26; Mick Loakes 15bl; Steven Sweet 6–7, 24bl, David Wright 12–13, 14, 15tr, 15mr, 16–17, 18–19, 21tr; Peter Wilkes (SGA) all cartoons.

CONTENTS

What is a desert?

Deserts are the driest parts of the world—places where it hardly ever rains. Most have less than 10 inches (25 centimeters) of rain per year—one tenth of the rain that falls every year in rainforests, the wettest parts of the world.

Deserts aren't only the world's driest places. They're also the windiest.

Are all deserts hot?

In many of the world's deserts, it is hot enough in the daytime to fry an egg on a rock. Not all deserts are like this, though. Some deserts have baking hot summers and freezing cold winters, while others are chilly all year long.

Even if you're heading for a hot desert, remember to pack a sweater. Although the daytime temperature can soar to over 140°F (40°C), it can drop to below 32°F (0°C) at night!

When it does rain in a desert, it can really rain! All of a desert's annual rain may fall in one tremendous storm over two or three days.

Even a sandy desert may be dotted with big rocks here and there. This huge boulder casts welcome shade during the hottest part of the day—great for people to shelter from the Sun's frazzling heat.

Are all deserts sandy?

No—some are gravelly, while others are rocky or even snowy. Antarctica is a cold, snowy desert, for example, where there is no rain and little sun.

Some deserts are a crazy paving pattern of dried-up salt flats—with a surface that's as hard as concrete.

Where is the world's biggest desert?

About one fifth of all the land on Earth is desert.

The largest desert in the whole world is the Sahara in North Africa. It's larger than Australia, and nearly the size of the entire United States.

Key to map

The driest deserts, where it hardly ever rains

Deserts that have enough rain for some plants to grow

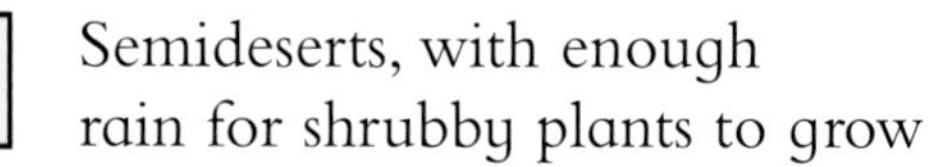

Semideserts, with enough rain for shrubby plants to grow

NORTH AMERICA

ATLANTIC OCEAN

Great Basin

Mojave

Sonoran

Chihuahuan

Equator

SOUTH AMERICA

Sechura

Atacama

Patagonian

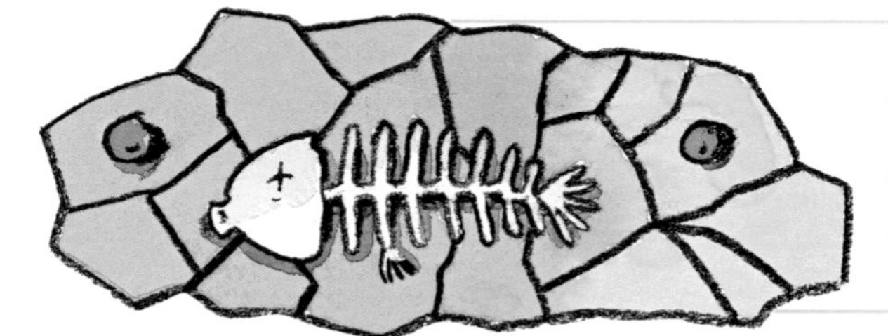

At 282 ft. (86m) below sea level, the Death Valley Desert is the lowest place in the U.S.

FOR SALE

One of the driest places in the world is South America's Atacama Desert. Parts of the Atacama had no rain at all between 1570 and 1971—that's 401 years!

Europe is the only continent without deserts.

The Empty Quarter in Arabia is the largest stretch of sandy desert outside of the Sahara. It's roughly the same size as France.

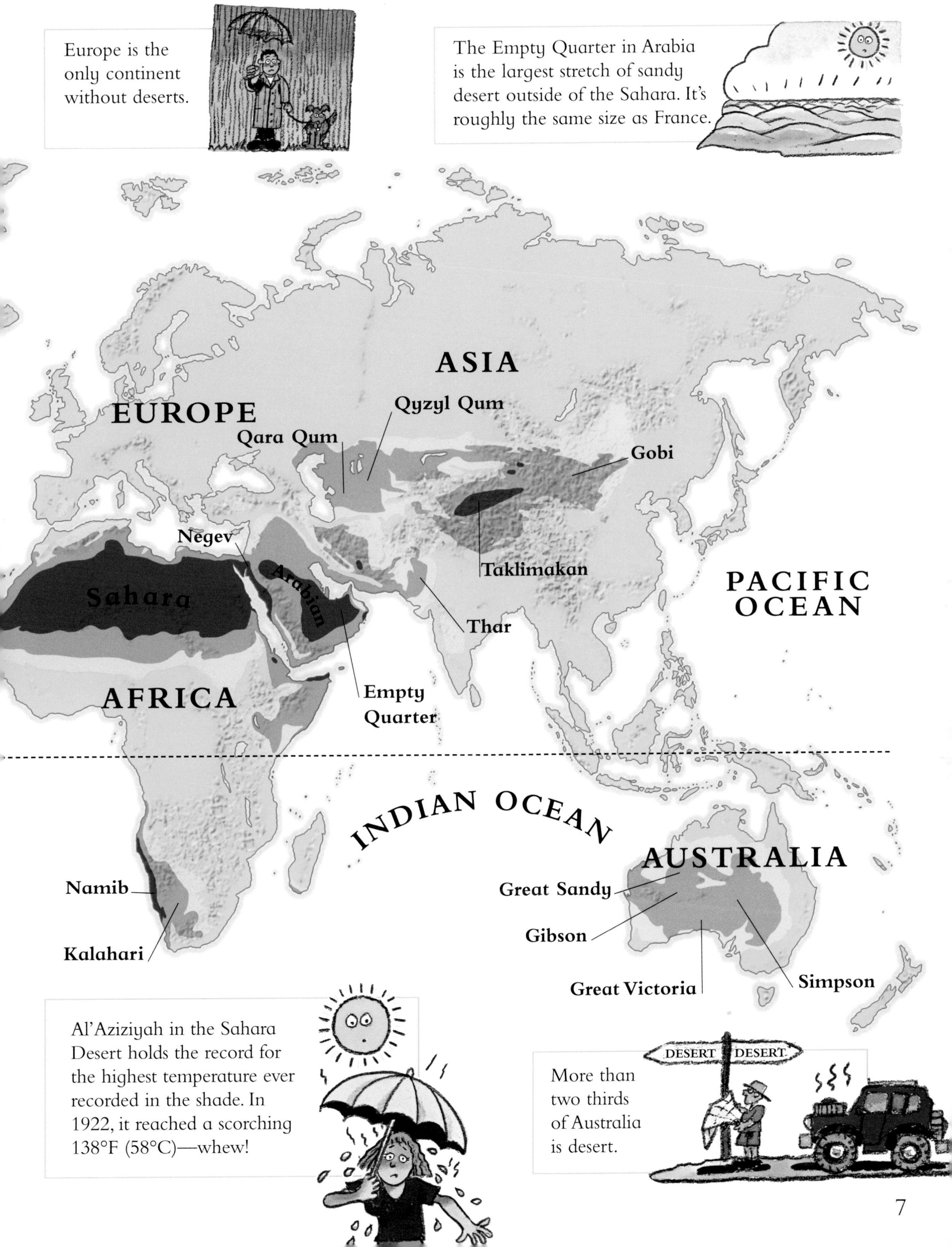

Al'Aziziyah in the Sahara Desert holds the record for the highest temperature ever recorded in the shade. In 1922, it reached a scorching 138°F (58°C)—whew!

More than two thirds of Australia is desert.

Why are deserts sandy?

Strong desert winds sometimes stir up huge clouds of sand. The wind-blown sand is powerful enough to strip the paint from a car.

Sandy deserts are formed mainly by the wind. As it howls across the land, the wind blasts at the rock, wearing it away. Slowly, the rock cracks into stones and pebbles which, over the ages, crumble into tiny sand grains.

How high are the tallest sand dunes?

Desert sand dunes come in many shapes and sizes, from camel-high bumps to steep-sided hills. The highest ones measure well over 900 ft. (300m)—more than twice as high as Egypt's tallest pyramid!

Where can you find mushroom-shaped rocks?

In a desert, of course! The wind carves rocks into all kinds of weird and wonderful shapes as it howls away at them.

At sunrise and sunset, the rocks and sand of North America's Painted Desert gleam a rainbow of colors—from blue and violet to golden yellow, brown, and red.

As the sand of a dune shifts and slips, it can give out strange booming or singing noises—spooky!

Some sand dunes are shaped like a crescent moon . . .

. . . while others look like a star.

An S-shaped sand dune is called a "seif," from the Arabic word for sword.

What is an oasis?

Although little water falls as rain in a desert, there are places where it rises to the surface from deep below the ground. If there's enough water all year long for plants to grow, we call that place an oasis.

A qanat is a deep underground tunnel dug out by people to bring water into the desert.

When is there water in a wadi?

A wadi is a desert river valley and most of the time it's as dry as a bone. When there's a rainstorm, however, the wadi fills quickly, and for a while it becomes a roaring, raging torrent of water.

Every year in the Australian desert town of Alice Springs, people race up the dry bed of the Todd river carrying bottomless boats!

How does sunlight trick desert travelers?

There's nothing a thirsty desert traveler wants to see more than water. But sometimes the shimmering blue pool up ahead isn't water at all—it's only an image of the sky. These tricks of the light are called mirages.

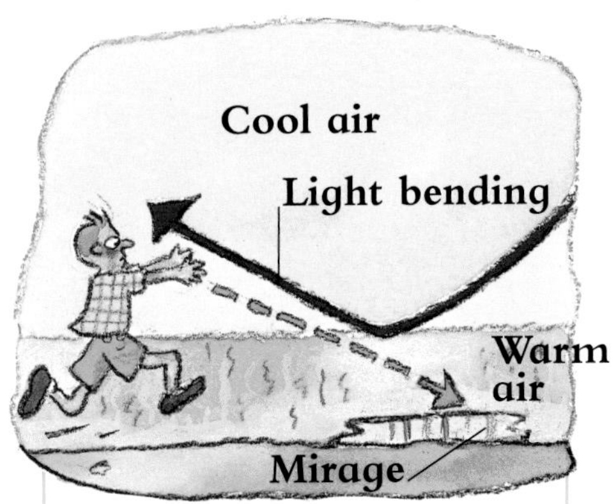

A mirage happens when sunlight is "bent" as it travels through hot air near the ground. The scientific name for this "bending" is refraction.

How do plants survive in deserts?

All living things need water to survive, so coping with dry desert weather is tough for plants and animals. Plants slurp up water through their roots, and some desert plants have very long roots that reach deep down under the ground.

The roots of the mesquite bush can tap water from as far as 100 ft. (30m) below the ground.

Why are cacti spiny?

A cactus's spines are like a barbed-wire fence. They protect the plant and stop most animals from eating it.

When desert plants do get water, they hang on to it. Some use their leaves like a water bank, while cacti store it in their fat, juicy stems.

When does the desert burst into flower?

The tallest cactus is the giant saguaro. It can grow to a massive 39 feet (12 meters)—taller than four camels!

Some desert plants don't grow at all unless it rains. When there is a storm, the seeds sprout, grow, and bloom within a matter of weeks—turning the dusty desert into a colorful flowering meadow.

Instead of spines, some cacti are camouflaged to hide them from animals. Stone cacti look just like pebbles.

The welwitschia of the Namib Desert looks more dead than alive. Don't be fooled, though. It can live for as long as 2,000 years.

How long can a camel last without drinking?

Camels can go for days without drinking water—weeks if they find enough juicy plants to eat. When a camel gets a drink, it can gulp down 211 pints (100 liters) in ten minutes.

There are two kinds of camel. An Arabian camel has one hump, and the Bactrian camel of Asia has two.

A camel can go for weeks without food because its hump is like a backpack, where food is stored as fat.

Many desert lizards store fat in their tails.

Which desert animals never drink?

Jerboas (right) and kangaroo rats don't drink. They get all the water they need from plant seeds and other food.

Foggy mornings give the darkling beetle of the Namib Desert all the water it needs. When it tips up its back, water droplets trickle down into its mouth.

Can toads live in the desert?

Nearly all other toads live in wet, watery places because they are amphibians—animals that have to lay their eggs in water.

One kind of toad has a smart way of surviving the desert drought. For most of the year, the American spadefoot toad keeps its cool in a deep underground burrow. It comes out only during the rainy season to lay its eggs.

The male sandgrouse is like a flying water bottle. When it finds a pool, it uses its fluffy breast feathers like a sponge to soak up water to carry home to its chicks.

How do desert foxes keep their cool?

The kit fox's big ears work like radiators, giving off heat and cooling down its body. They also help it listen out for enemies such as hyenas.

The jack rabbit is another desert animal with big ears to help it stay cool.

Which animal has its own sun parasol?

Unlike most other small desert animals, ground squirrels spend their days out in the sun. They shelter from the midday heat under their own sun parasols—their tails!

Many ground squirrels also use their tails for signalling to one another if danger is near.

The golden mole spends most of its life burrowing through the sand. It can tunnel more than 2.5 miles (4 kilometers) in one night.

Many desert animals have light-colored fur, which helps them stay cool by reflecting sunlight.

Why do desert animals love the dark?

The elf owl shelters from the hot desert sunlight in a hole in a tall saguaro cactus.

It's a lot cooler out of the sun than in it, so many small desert animals shelter from the daytime heat in underground burrows. They come out to hunt for food at night, or in the early morning and evening.

How do rattlesnakes kill their prey?

An attacking rattlesnake is lightning fast. It opens its mouth wide, swings its fangs forward, then bites to inject a deadly poison through them. Small victims die within seconds.

The rattlesnake is named after the rattling noise it makes by shaking the tip of its tail.

Which desert lizards are poisonous?

Hundreds of different lizards live in deserts, but only two are poisonous—the U.S.'s gila monster and the Mexican beaded lizard. Don't worry, though. These lizards use their poison mainly to protect themselves from enemies, not to attack prey.

Why do scorpions have a sting in their tail?

The chuckwalla lizard protects itself from enemies by squeezing into a crack in the rock and puffing up its body with air. It is as difficult to pull out as a cork from a bottle.

Scorpions inject poison through their tails, but only if they're very annoyed. Usually, they use only their claws to catch and kill prey. Scorpions have small eyes and don't see all that well, so they usually track prey using their senses of touch and smell.

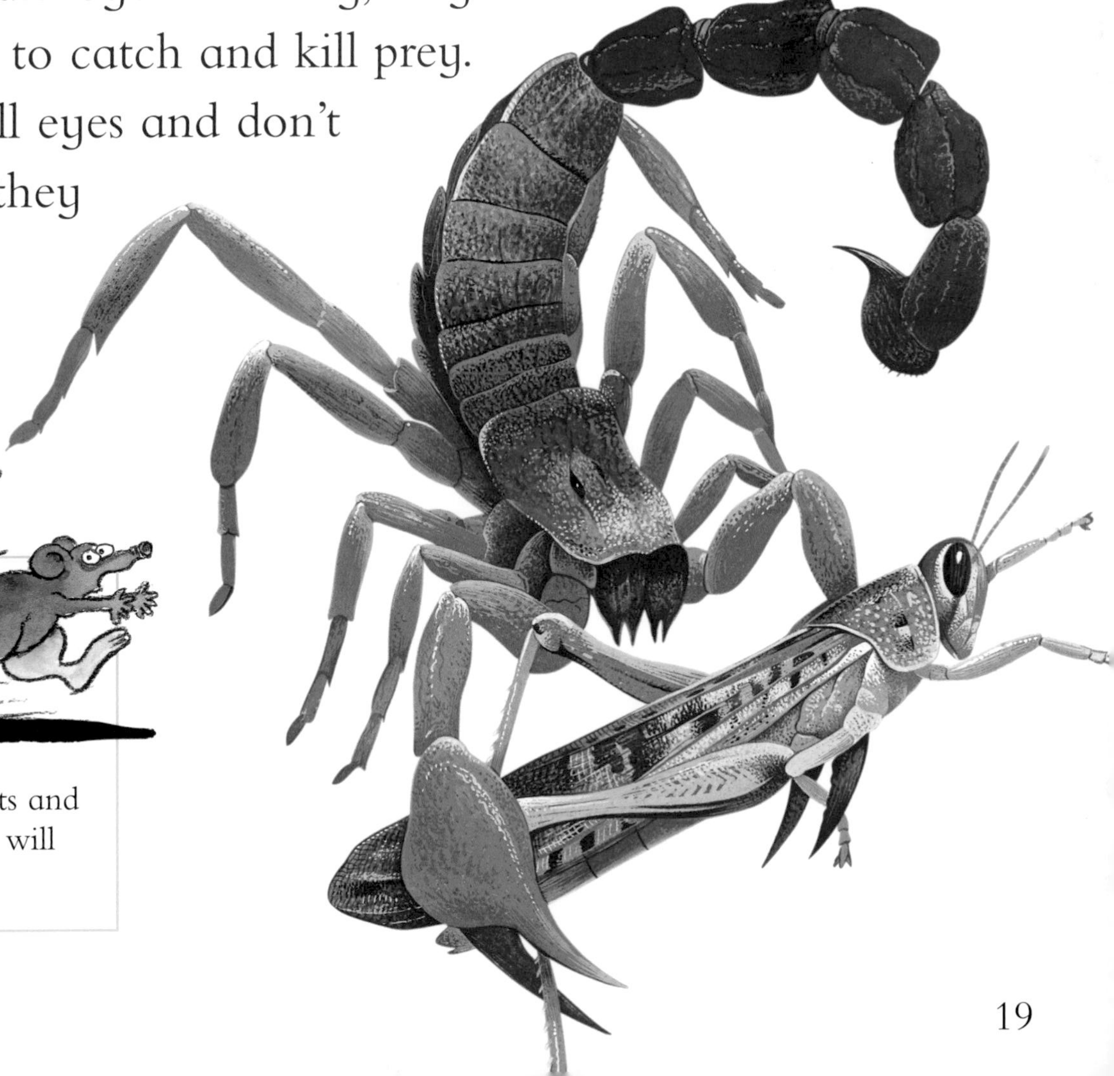

Scorpions mainly eat insects and spiders, but large scorpions will eat lizards and mice.

How do people live in the desert?

Desert survival is all about finding enough water and food to stay alive. Some desert people move from place to place all of the time, following good sources of water and food. These traveling people are called nomads.

The San people of the Kalahari Desert are so expert at tracking down water, they can find small pockets of it under the sand. They suck up the water through a reed straw and store it in an ostrich shell.

What do nomadic people find to eat?

Few desert nomads hunt for wild food these days. Instead, most keep their own herds so they can drink the animals' milk or make it into cheese.

Who ate ants?

In the past, the nomadic Aboriginal people of the Australian deserts survived entirely by hunting and finding wild food—everything from kangaroos to lizards, insects, and plants. Sweet things were rare, so finding a nest of honeypot ants was an extraspecial treat.

When rains make the desert bloom, honeypot ants feed on sugary nectar from flowers. Some ants store the nectar in their bodies, turning themselves into living honey pots.

The Tuareg are nomadic herders who live in the Sahara Desert. Their name means the "people of the veil"—the men's faces are almost completely hidden by their veil-like turbans.

Nomadic people do not move on every day—only when they need fresh supplies of water or food.

Why do desert people build mud houses?

Mud is a fantastic building material. Homes with thick mud walls stay cool inside when the sun is baking hot outdoors, and warm inside if the weather turns cold. Best of all, mud is dirt cheap—all you have to do is dig it up.

Homes can be built from layers of clay mud, or from bricks made by mixing mud with straw or animal hair.

Are there towns in the desert?

There certainly are. Although, in the past, thousands of desert people led a nomadic way of life, very few do today. Most live around oases in river valleys such as the Nile or on the desert fringe.

What is a yurt?

Travelers need portable homes, and yurts are the traditional round tents of the nomadic Mongol people of the Gobi Desert. They are made from wooden poles covered with felt made from sheep's wool.

The tents of the nomadic Bedouin people of the Middle East are covered with cloth woven from goats' hairs.

Where do people paint with sand?

In South America's Nazca Desert, more than 1,200 years ago, people scratched huge pictures of birds and other animals into the stony ground.

The Navajo people create beautiful paintings with colored sands for healing rites and other traditional ceremonies. They live in the southeast of the U.S.'s Great Basin Desert.

Why did Australian explorers import camels?

In February 1861, Robert Burke and William Wills became the first settlers to cross Australia from south to north. They wanted camels to carry their supplies because their route took them straight through the deserts in the heart of the continent. But because camels aren't Australian animals, the explorers had to import them from Afghanistan.

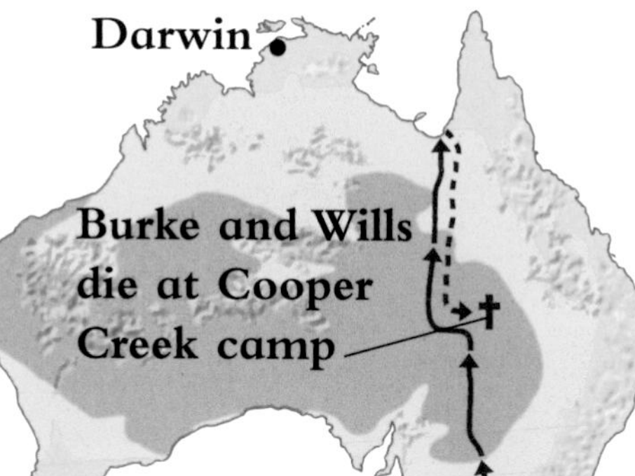

Sadly, Burke and Wills both starved to death on the return journey south. Their companion, John King, survived.

Who was the first to make it across the Sahara in a microlight?

British explorer Christina Dodwell was the first to do it, in the 1980s. She flew a mammoth 6,800 mi. (11,000km) across Africa.

Which desert explorer carried water in his boots?

Swede Sven Hedin nearly died of thirst when he traveled across Asia's Taklimakan Desert in the 1890s. When he at last stumbled across water, two of his companions were dead and the third had given up walking hours before. Hedin saved the third man's life by carrying water back to him in his boots.

When Chinese monk Hsuan Tsang set off alone into the Gobi Desert in the 600s, almost the first thing he did was drop his water bag. He was saved by his horse, which smelled grass growing around a water hole and led him to safety.

Where do cars race across the desert?

Briton Andy Green became the world's fastest man on wheels in October 1997, when his jet-propelled car *ThrustSSC* reached a mind-boggling 763 mph (1,228kmph). He set the record on the smooth flat surface of North America's Black Rock Desert.

Every year, between 1979 and 2007, racing drivers diced with death during the Paris to Dakar rally which took them through the Sahara Desert. Since 2009 the race has taken place in South America.

The *Opportunity* rover was tested in U.S. deserts before its launch to Mars, where it landed in 2004.

Why are space rovers tested in the desert?

Being in a desert is the nearest you can get on Earth to experiencing what it's like on Mars. And that makes a desert the ideal place for putting a space rover through its paces.

Which is the world's toughest foot race?

You have to be made of tough stuff to enter the Marathon of the Sands. This foot race takes place in the Sahara Desert, with runners covering around 140 miles (230 kilometers) in six days. That's farther than five normal marathons!

Although the temperature can reach 113°F (45°C) at midday, the Saharan runners have to carry food, clothes, and everything else they need—apart from a tent.

Camels are raced like horses in the Arabian deserts. Their top speed is well over 18 miles (30 kilometers) per hour.

Is there treasure in the desert?

Yes—gold, silver, and diamonds have all been found in deserts. One of the world's largest diamond mines is in the Kalahari Desert.

What is black gold?

People often call oil "black gold," because it is one of our planet's most valuable natural resources. Finding it on their land has made individual people and entire countries very, very wealthy.

Salt was as precious as gold in ancient times, and there were salt mines deep in the Sahara Desert.

Much of the world's oil is drilled from rocks deep beneath the Arabian deserts.

How can deserts give us clean energy?

Treasure doesn't always glitter. In 1923, American archaeologists were the first to discover fossilized dinosaur eggs in the Gobi Desert. The eggs were sold for thousands of dollars.

Solar power stations are places where the Sun's heat is used to generate electricity. They are much cleaner than a power station that burns oil or coal, and hot deserts are the ideal places to build them.

One of the world's largest solar power stations is in the U.S.'s Mojave Desert.

Did grass ever grow in the Sahara Desert?

Climates change gradually. Thousands of years ago the Sahara was much wetter, with grass to feed animals. We know this because there are fossils and ancient rock paintings which show that cows, antelopes, giraffes, and elephants once lived there.

What turns green land into desert?

Overfarming is a major culprit. Plant roots bind soil, stopping the wind from blowing it away. When people farm too many animals on the desert fringe, the animals eat all the plants, the soil disappears, and the land becomes desert.

Deserts also spread if the climate changes, bringing much less rain.

The rock paintings also show people swimming in ancient Saharan rivers and lakes, as well as water animals such as hippopotamuses and crocodiles.

Can deserts be changed into green fields?

Huge watering projects are one way of turning deserts green again. In parts of North Africa the sand is dotted with round fields created by gigantic spinning sprinklers.

In some parts of Arabia, the leftovers from refining oil are sprayed on sand dunes. The gray, muddy mixture holds water, allowing plants to grow.

Index